THE ILLUSION OF AI

Truths You're Not Being Told

How Companies Are Misleading You with
AI and What That Could Mean for Your
Future

MUSKAN BEN

TABLE OF CONTENT

INTRODUCTION

Unveiling the AI Mirage

In today's world, AI is everywhere. From the moment we wake up to the time we go to bed, we interact with it in ways we don't even realize. AI is in our phones, in our cars, in our social media feeds, and increasingly, in the products we buy and the services we use. It's often promised as the future—a game-changer that will revolutionize every aspect of our lives. Companies tout it as the key to efficiency, innovation, and progress.

But what if that's not the whole truth? What if the AI we're being sold isn't as magical or revolutionary as we've been led to believe? What if, behind all the buzzwords, the sleek advertisements, and the polished presentations, there's something much darker lurking in the background?

Welcome to the world of AI deception.

For decades, we've been promised that AI will make our lives easier, safer, and more productive. We've been sold a vision of self-driving cars, fully automated shopping experiences, and intelligent assistants that understand our every need. We've been told that AI will solve problems we've struggled with for centuries—disease, hunger, inequality. It's hard to escape the hype, especially when the biggest tech companies in the world are pushing it harder than ever.

But behind this facade of perfection lies a story of overhyped technology, manipulated promises, and an industry that's more concerned with selling a vision than delivering a reality. In fact, much of what we think is AI—what we see and hear in the media and advertising—is far from it. It's an illusion, carefully crafted by companies that are more interested in riding the wave of AI's popularity than in actually delivering on its promises.

This book will pull back the curtain on the AI revolution and expose the truth about what's really going on. From the so-called "magic" behind Amazon's Just Walk Out technology to the AI-washing tactics used by major corporations to inflate their stock prices, we'll uncover the hidden realities that tech giants don't want you to see. We'll show you the people behind the scenes, the manual labor disguised as automation, and the dark side of a future we've all been sold.

You might be wondering: Why does it matter? Why should we care about the truth behind AI's promises? Well, because the consequences of this deception are more significant than you might think. The AI revolution is not just about technology—it's about power, money, and control. It's about how companies manipulate the very fabric of society by promising utopian futures while leaving us with a dystopian present.

If you've ever felt like something didn't quite add up with all the AI hype—or if you've ever wondered why things aren't as seamless as they're made out to be—this book is for you. You'll discover how AI is being used to mislead consumers, investors, and the public, and how the real impact of AI might not be what you expect.

Are you ready to uncover the truth? Let's dive in.

CHAPTER 1

The Origins of AI Deception – From the Mechanical Turk to Amazon's Just Walk Out

The world of technology is no stranger to illusions—grand promises that excite the imagination, only to eventually reveal themselves as something far less extraordinary. In fact, one of the earliest and most notable examples of this kind of deception dates back to 1770, with the invention of the Mechanical Turk.

The Mechanical Turk, a chess-playing machine created by Hungarian inventor Wolfgang von Kempelen, captured the attention of Europe for nearly a century. To the untrained eye, it was a marvel—an automaton that could play chess against human opponents, even defeating famous players like Napoleon Bonaparte and Benjamin Franklin. The idea that a machine could outthink and outplay the best minds of the day was nothing short of revolutionary. The Turk was the epitome of technological wonder.

But there was one small problem: it wasn't a machine at all. Behind the intricate clockwork and moving gears, there was a human operator hidden inside the machine, controlling the Turk's movements. The chess-playing robot was nothing more than an elaborate hoax. Von Kempelen had effectively fooled the world into believing that a machine had the capacity for intellect, when in reality, it was all just a clever illusion. Despite being exposed as a fraud, the Turk continued to captivate audiences for decades, highlighting humanity's penchant for believing in the miraculous possibilities of technology.

Fast forward to 2016, and the world was introduced to another so-called technological breakthrough—Amazon's "Just Walk Out" technology. This was marketed as the future of shopping: a frictionless, fully automated system where customers could simply grab items off the shelves and walk out without ever needing to stop at a checkout counter. Amazon promoted it as an AI-powered solution that would change the way people shop, using computer vision, sensor fusion, and deep learning to track purchases in real time. The company's sleek advertising painted a picture of a future where the tedious task of checking out was eliminated entirely, replaced by a seamless, AI-driven experience.

In reality, however, Amazon's "Just Walk Out" system was not as autonomous as advertised. While the technology did indeed rely on cameras and sensors, it was still heavily reliant on human workers. Thousands of people were watching live footage from cameras in the stores, manually labeling data and ensuring the system functioned properly. In other words, Amazon's seemingly "AI-powered" checkout system was not fully automated at all. It was yet another example of human labor being hidden behind the illusion of advanced technology. The use of real humans in the background undermined the glossy picture painted by Amazon, raising questions about the ethics of presenting such a system as an entirely AI-driven experience.

The parallels between the Mechanical Turk and Amazon's Just Walk Out technology are striking. Both were presented to the public as technological marvels that would revolutionize industries, but both hid the truth about their limitations. In the case of the Turk, it was a human under the table; with Amazon, it was thousands of workers behind the scenes. Both examples exploited the public's desire to believe in the extraordinary capabilities of machines, capitalizing on the allure of automation and artificial intelligence.

These deceptions, both historical and modern, have a profound effect on public perception. They shape how we view the potential of AI and influence our expectations of what technology can and should do. The reality is that AI is still far from the level of autonomy that many companies claim. These grand promises of fully automated systems, whether in chess-playing machines or retail technology, often fall short of the truth. Yet, these illusions continue to captivate, leaving us wondering what other technological promises might be hiding behind the curtain.

In many ways, these deceptions reflect a common thread: the human desire to create a world where machines can think, feel, and act independently. This vision is so compelling that we are willing to overlook the cracks in the facade, even when the truth is right in front of us. As we move forward into the AI revolution, we must ask ourselves: how many other "mechanical turks" are out there, hidden behind the shiny promises of advanced technology?

CHAPTER 2

AI-Washing – The Fake Buzz Around AI

AI-washing is a term that has become increasingly relevant in today's tech-driven world, where the very mention of artificial intelligence can have a profound impact on stock prices, investment, and public perception. But what exactly does it mean? Simply put, AI-washing is the practice of companies overstating or misrepresenting their use of AI to create the illusion of innovation, sophistication, and forward-thinking. It's a deliberate attempt to ride the wave of AI hype without actually delivering any real, meaningful AI products or advancements.

In the fast-paced world of business, AI has become a buzzword—a catchphrase that is tossed around in boardrooms, on investor calls, and in marketing materials. The term "AI" has become synonymous with success, efficiency, and a bright future. But just like any other trend, companies have learned that slapping the AI label onto a product or service can generate significant attention, raise stock prices, and attract investors. The real challenge, however, is that in many cases, these companies are not using AI at all—or at least not in the ways they claim.

Take the case of Goldman Sachs, for instance. According to their reports, a staggering 36% of S&P 500 companies mentioned AI in their earnings reports, showcasing their commitment to innovation and technological progress. However, when analysts dug deeper, they found that many of these companies had little to no actual AI integration in their business models. The companies had simply adopted the language of AI, attaching the label to existing products or processes without any substantial changes or breakthroughs. This "AI-washing" allowed them to capitalize on the trend and lure in investors who were eager to be part of the next big technological revolution.

Then, there's the case of Delia, a Canadian investment firm that made headlines for its claims of developing AI to predict upcoming industry trends. According to Delia, their AI-driven algorithms would be able to analyze massive amounts of data to identify patterns and forecast the future with unprecedented accuracy. The firm marketed itself as a pioneer in the AI space, attracting significant investments and attention. But when regulators began to scrutinize Delia's operations, they found that the firm wasn't using AI at all. Instead, Delia relied on traditional methods of data analysis, repackaged under the guise of AI to attract investors and create the illusion of cutting-edge technology. The firm was fined by the SEC for false advertising and misleading claims, a stark reminder of how easily companies can manipulate the narrative around AI.

These examples illustrate the growing pressure on companies to claim that they are utilizing AI in order to remain relevant in an increasingly tech-centric world. As AI becomes more ingrained in the fabric of modern business, there's a growing sense that if you're not using AI, you're falling behind. This has led to a rise in AI-related investments, with companies— large and small—rushing to position themselves as key players in the AI revolution. But the rush to claim AI credentials often results in companies stretching the truth or making exaggerated claims about what their technology can actually do.

This pressure to "jump on the AI bandwagon" has created a marketplace where many businesses are more concerned with appearing innovative than with actually implementing transformative AI technology. In this environment, it's easy for companies to throw the term "AI" around in an attempt to secure funding, attract attention, and boost their brand image. But the result is a flood of half-baked AI products, misleading claims, and ultimately, a diluted understanding of what AI is and what it can do.

AI-washing not only undermines consumer trust, but it also damages the credibility of the tech industry as a whole. It creates an environment where real innovation is overshadowed by inflated promises and exaggerated marketing. And as we continue to navigate the AI landscape, it's crucial that we remain vigilant—questioning the claims made by companies, demanding transparency, and insisting on genuine technological advancements rather than hollow buzzwords.

The rise of AI-related investments and the pressure to jump on the AI bandwagon has led to a dangerous trend: companies using the term "AI" as a shortcut to success without actually delivering on the promises that come with it. AI-washing might sound like a clever marketing tactic, but in reality, it's a disservice to consumers, investors, and the future of AI itself. It's time to look beyond the buzzwords, separate fact from fiction, and hold companies accountable for the true potential of the technology they claim to embrace.

CHAPTER 3

Behind the Curtain – How AI is Really Powered

Behind the curtain of every so-called "AI-powered" system lies a story that the public rarely hears. While artificial intelligence is often presented as the pinnacle of technological progress, a closer look reveals that much of what we believe to be automated is, in fact, heavily reliant on human labor. This is the hidden truth behind the AI revolution—the often-invisible hands that make the magic happen, the workers who label data, train models, and correct mistakes long before the systems can function independently.

One of the most striking examples of this hidden labor is the process of data labeling, a critical step in the development of machine learning algorithms. AI systems, especially those that rely on deep learning, require vast amounts of labeled data to function effectively. In simple terms, data labeling is the process of tagging data—images, text, videos, or any other form of input—so that an AI system can learn from it. For instance, to train a self-driving car, thousands of images need to be labeled with information about road signs, pedestrians, and other vehicles. Without this foundational work, AI algorithms would have no context to understand the world around them.

But here's the catch: while AI may appear to operate autonomously, much of this data labeling is done by humans. According to industry reports, manual labor accounts for a significant portion of the work required to train AI systems. This labor-intensive process is typically outsourced to low-wage workers in developing countries, where the work is done in a highly controlled environment to ensure accuracy and consistency.

Take Amazon's "Just Walk Out" technology, for example. When Amazon first rolled out its supposedly fully automated system for checkout-free shopping, it was marketed as a groundbreaking leap forward in AI-powered retail. The system relied on computer vision, sensor fusion, and machine learning to track purchases, so customers could simply pick up items and leave the store without ever scanning them at a checkout. On the surface, it seemed like a true showcase of AI's capabilities. The future of shopping had arrived.

But in reality, Amazon's system was not as autonomous as it appeared. Behind the scenes, thousands of people were working in the shadows, labeling data and ensuring that the system worked smoothly. According to reports, Amazon employed 1,000 workers in India who reviewed video footage from the stores, manually identifying and tagging transactions that the system couldn't process on its own. These workers were essential in the early stages of training the system, providing feedback, and fixing errors that arose. The reality was that while customers experienced the convenience of automated checkout, human labor was responsible for making sure the system didn't collapse.

This is a prime example of how companies fail to disclose the human effort required to support their so-called AI systems. Instead, they present an image of sleek, fully autonomous technology, masking the true complexity of what's involved. When Amazon promoted its "Just Walk Out" technology as being driven by AI, it didn't tell consumers about the hidden workforce that made it possible. This omission led to a distorted view of what AI could actually achieve—reinforcing the myth that AI was operating without any human involvement.

The ethical implications of hiding the truth about AI's capabilities are far-reaching. When companies market AI technology as fully autonomous, they not only mislead consumers but also create unrealistic expectations. People begin to believe that AI is capable of much more than it is, leading to a false sense of security and overreliance on technology that isn't yet ready to stand on its own.

Moreover, the use of low-wage workers in countries like India raises serious questions about the ethics of outsourcing critical work that supports these technologies. The labor behind AI development is often invisible to the public, and yet it is the backbone of what makes these systems function. By presenting AI as an entirely self-sufficient solution, companies fail to acknowledge the human cost of their "cutting-edge" technology, creating a false narrative that damages both public trust and the workers who are doing the grunt work.

As we move forward in an increasingly AI-driven world, it's crucial that we question the hype and demand transparency from companies. The reality is that AI is still in its early stages, and much of the "autonomy" we see is a carefully constructed illusion. Companies need to be upfront about the labor and resources required to make their AI systems work, rather than hiding behind a veil of technological wizardry. The truth behind AI is far more complex—and far more human—than the glossy advertisements let on.

In the end, the ethical implications of misrepresenting AI's true capabilities are significant. When companies refuse to acknowledge the hidden human labor behind their AI systems, they not only undermine the trust of consumers but also fail to give proper credit to the workers who are doing the real work. The future of AI is not just about technology; it's about transparency, fairness, and the ethical responsibility of those creating it. Until we address the truth about how AI is powered, we will continue to live in an illusion where the machines are seen as more capable than they really are, and the human effort behind them remains unseen.

CHAPTER 4

The Consequences of AI Overhype – Trust Issues and Dystopian Futures

The rise of artificial intelligence has been accompanied by a wave of grand promises—visions of a future where machines think, learn, and work alongside us, making life easier, more efficient, and more productive. Companies have touted AI as the solution to everything from climate change to poverty, and many of us have eagerly embraced the idea of a world transformed by these intelligent systems. But as the reality of AI's capabilities begins to clash with the hype, we're starting to see the consequences of overpromising what this technology can actually do.

One of the most significant effects of this overhyping is the erosion of public trust. When a company or product is advertised as revolutionary, promising to solve problems in ways we've never seen before, expectations skyrocket. People imagine a world where AI-powered systems solve every problem, automate every task, and improve every aspect of their lives. However, when those promises fail to materialize, when AI doesn't live up to its glowing advertisements, trust begins to break down.

This isn't just about disappointment—this is a deep loss of confidence in technology and the companies behind it. The public begins to feel misled, and the feeling that AI has been sold to them as a shiny, unattainable dream leads to a sense of betrayal. For investors, the stakes are even higher. When expectations are built on the notion that AI will be the next great leap forward, and those expectations aren't met, it can result in a massive backlash. Companies that have overpromised the capabilities of AI may see their stock prices plummet, their reputations tarnished, and their future prospects threatened. This can lead to a broader loss of faith in the entire AI sector, a phenomenon that is becoming more pronounced as the gap between AI's promises and reality continues to widen.

But perhaps the most unsettling consequence of AI overhype is the dystopian future that could unfold if companies continue to push the narrative that AI will replace human workers in vast numbers. There's a popular mantra often repeated by advocates of AI: "AI will create more jobs than it destroys." The idea is that while AI might automate certain tasks, it will also open up new opportunities and create entirely new industries. In theory, this sounds reassuring—a future where technology frees us from mundane, repetitive work and allows us to pursue more creative and meaningful endeavors.

But the reality may be far different. As AI technology continues to improve, there's an increasing risk that it won't create the new jobs that we were promised. Instead, it could lead to massive job displacement, particularly in sectors like manufacturing, retail, and customer service, where automation is already starting to take hold. The idea that AI will simply "augment" human labor is at odds with the economic pressures many companies face to cut costs and maximize efficiency. The more sophisticated AI becomes, the more likely it is that human workers will be replaced, not augmented. This could result in a world where vast numbers of people find themselves without stable work, struggling to adapt to an economy that no longer has a place for them.

This presents a stark contrast to the promises made by tech companies. While they sell AI as a tool to improve our lives, the reality could be a future where technology becomes a threat to our livelihoods rather than a tool for liberation. The very idea that we are creating systems meant to enhance human life, only to end up replacing humans in the process, feels like a cruel paradox. It's a scenario where the AI revolution—promised as a golden age of efficiency and prosperity—becomes a nightmare for those who are left behind by automation.

All of this is further compounded by the Gartner Hype Cycle, a well-known framework used to track the progress of emerging technologies. The cycle predicts that any new technology goes through a predictable sequence of stages, from the Innovation Trigger (when the idea first emerges) to the Peak of Inflated Expectations, then to the Trough of Disillusionment, followed by the Slope of Enlightenment, and finally, the Plateau of Productivity. In the case of AI, we're currently at the Peak of Inflated Expectations—a point where the technology has been overhyped to such an extent that it seems as if AI will solve all of humanity's problems. But the crash is coming, and when it happens, we'll likely enter the Trough of Disillusionment, where the reality of AI's limitations becomes clear.

This period of disillusionment could be marked by massive investment losses, widespread disappointment, and a harsh re-evaluation of what AI can realistically achieve. For consumers and investors, it will feel like the rug has been pulled out from under them. The dream of a seamless, AI-driven future will seem farther away than ever, leaving us to question whether AI will ever live up to the hype—or if it was always destined to be another overblown technological fad.

The consequences of AI overhype are more than just economic—they are societal. When the promises of AI fail to materialize, it creates a divide between those who are in the know and those who have been left behind. For workers whose jobs are displaced by AI, for investors who bet on the wrong companies, and for consumers who expected life-changing innovation, the fallout will be felt for years to come. AI, once seen as the great hope of the future, may become a symbol of disappointment, mistrust, and inequality.

As we look ahead to the coming years, the AI revolution could take many forms. If companies are willing to acknowledge the limitations of AI, to be transparent about what it can and cannot do, we might still see it fulfill its potential as a transformative tool. But if the hype continues unchecked, and if we fail to address the ethical and social implications of AI's widespread adoption, we may very well find ourselves in a dystopian future where technology has taken more than it has given.

CHAPTER 5

AI in the Real World – Missteps, Failures, and Unintended Consequences

In the rush to promote AI as the solution to every modern problem, many companies have launched products that they claimed would revolutionize the way we live and work. However, the reality of these AI systems often falls short of expectations, leading to failures that not only disappoint users but also raise serious questions about the capabilities and ethics of artificial intelligence. These missteps, while humorous or embarrassing in some cases, have far-reaching implications for the future of AI development and its place in our lives.

One of the most infamous examples of AI failure comes from DPD, a parcel delivery company that deployed an AI-powered chatbot to handle customer inquiries. On paper, the idea seemed like a good one: an automated system that could quickly provide information, handle complaints, and answer questions, all without the need for a human representative.

However, the reality was anything but seamless. When customers interacted with the DPD chatbot, they found themselves met with irrelevant, nonsensical responses. In one particularly egregious example, a customer asked the chatbot about the status of their delivery, only to receive a poem that had nothing to do with their inquiry—followed by a string of profanity aimed at the company itself.

The chatbot's failure wasn't just an inconvenience for the customer—it was a public relations disaster for DPD. The company's attempt to streamline its customer service with AI ended up creating more frustration than solutions, and the embarrassing interaction quickly went viral. The chatbot's failure highlighted the limitations of AI when it comes to handling complex, real-world tasks. Despite its potential to improve efficiency, AI still struggles with the nuances of human language, context, and customer service, especially in cases where empathy and understanding are required.

This incident serves as a stark reminder that AI, while promising, is still far from perfect. The problem wasn't just that the AI failed to provide a helpful response—it was that the system wasn't equipped to handle the diversity of human interaction. This led to a crisis of trust for DPD, as customers were left questioning whether the company was capable of implementing technology that was supposed to improve their experience. The backlash wasn't just from the customer who received the poem—it was from anyone who heard the story and wondered if AI could really be trusted to handle something as important as their deliveries.

Another striking example of AI gone wrong comes from Australia, where a group of academics used an AI-generated complaint to submit a report to the Australian government. The academics, in an effort to save time, decided to use an AI tool to help generate their submission against four major Australian banks. However, the AI went a step too far—it not only fabricated information, including scandalous claims about the banks, but it also implicated a government department (the Department of Education) in activities that had nothing to do with the complaint. The AI-generated report was riddled with falsehoods, inaccuracies, and made-up events, leading to a public embarrassment for the academics involved.

The fallout from this incident was swift. The report's reliance on AI to generate the content led to significant credibility damage for the academics and their institution. The AI had misrepresented facts, generating false claims that put reputations at risk. In this case, the use of AI didn't save time—it backfired, making the academics appear reckless and irresponsible. The incident raised important questions about the ethics of using AI to produce content that could have serious consequences, especially when the technology fails to verify the accuracy of the information it generates.

These examples—DPD's disastrous chatbot and the fabricated AI-generated report—underscore a fundamental truth about AI in the real world: technology doesn't always live up to the hype. While AI can be a powerful tool, it is far from infallible. Missteps like these damage the credibility of AI developers and erode the trust that consumers place in these systems. In both cases, customers and the public at large were left feeling misled and skeptical about the promises of AI. Instead of seeing the future of technology, they saw the limitations and flaws of a system still in its infancy.

The damage to consumer confidence that comes from these AI failures is significant. Trust is a vital component of any relationship between a business and its customers, and when AI systems fail, that trust can be shattered in an instant. Consumers expect AI to enhance their lives, to be a reliable assistant that can handle tasks and solve problems. When these expectations are unmet, it doesn't just lead to frustration—it leads to disillusionment, where people begin to question whether AI can really deliver on its promises at all.

These failures also have broader implications for the AI industry. When a high-profile AI product fails, it sends a ripple effect through the entire sector, causing potential investors, users, and developers to reconsider the feasibility and practicality of the technology. If AI systems continue to fail in these high-profile ways, there's a risk that the credibility of AI as a whole could be permanently damaged. The initial excitement around AI could quickly turn to skepticism, and companies that rely on AI to differentiate themselves might find that their investments in the technology were misguided.

For AI to succeed in the long term, developers must learn from these failures. The technology is still evolving, and it's clear that it has vast potential. But companies must be honest about its limitations, and consumers must be realistic about what AI can and can't do. There's no shame in acknowledging that AI is still learning, still growing, and still far from perfect. The key is to temper expectations, promote transparency, and recognize that AI, like any other technology, has its flaws—and it's okay to take the time to fix them before rolling out systems that promise the world.

CHAPTER 6

The AI Bubble – Are We Heading for Another Dotcom Crash?

The story of technological innovation is often one of extreme highs and crushing lows. In the late 1990s, the world witnessed the dotcom bubble, a period of speculative investment driven by the belief that the internet would transform every industry and solve every problem. Companies with little more than a catchy name and a vague business plan were valued in the billions, and investors flocked to them, eager to be part of what they believed was the next big thing. But when the bubble burst, billions of dollars were lost, and many of the so-called "tech giants" collapsed under the weight of their unrealistic valuations. The dotcom crash serves as a cautionary tale of how hype can distort the true value of technology.

Fast forward to today, and we find ourselves in the midst of another technological frenzy: AI. Much like the dotcom bubble, the world has become enamored with the promise of AI. Companies are touting AI as the future of everything— from business automation to healthcare to entertainment—

and investors are eagerly pouring money into AI startups and established tech giants alike. The question is: Are we heading for another crash? Is the current AI hype nothing more than another bubble waiting to burst?

There are striking similarities between the AI boom and the dotcom bubble. Both are fueled by the belief that a single technology can change the world. In the case of the dotcom era, it was the internet; today, it's artificial intelligence. In both cases, companies are overvalued based on exaggerated promises about the transformative power of the technology. In the dotcom era, companies without any real revenue or business model were valued in the billions. Today, AI companies are often valued based on the belief that their technology will eventually dominate entire industries, despite the fact that many of these companies have not yet proven their ability to deliver on those promises.

One of the clearest signs that we may be heading toward another bubble is the record corporate investments flowing into AI. Companies like Google, Microsoft, and Amazon are pouring billions of dollars into AI research and development. Startups that claim to be working on the next big breakthrough in AI are raising astronomical sums of money, often with little more than a prototype or a vague business plan. Investors are so eager to cash in on the AI revolution that they're overlooking the inherent risks and uncertainties that come with such speculative investments.

Take Nvidia, for example. The company's stock price has surged in recent years, largely due to the growing demand for its graphics processing units (GPUs), which are essential for training AI models. Nvidia's stock has become a proxy for the AI boom, with investors betting that the company will benefit from the increasing reliance on AI across industries. In fact, Nvidia's market value has skyrocketed, driven in large part by the AI hype. While Nvidia's products are certainly in demand, the question remains: is its stock price inflated due to speculative investment in AI, or is it truly worth the skyrocketing valuation?

Nvidia's example highlights a key issue with AI investments: the risk of overvaluation. Just as the dotcom bubble saw companies with little more than a website and a dream being valued in the billions, today's AI companies are often valued based on the promise of future success rather than their actual current performance. This speculative investment creates a dangerous environment where valuations are based on hype, not substance. If AI fails to live up to its lofty expectations—or if companies aren't able to turn their AI breakthroughs into profitable businesses—we could see a major correction, similar to what happened in the dotcom crash.

Mark Cuban, the billionaire investor and owner of the Dallas Mavericks, has weighed in on the AI hype, offering a nuanced perspective on whether AI is truly a bubble or a new technology cycle. Cuban has acknowledged that while AI has the potential to revolutionize many industries, he believes that much of the current hype is overblown. He points out that the technology is still in its early stages, and while it may eventually transform sectors like healthcare and manufacturing, it's not going to happen overnight. According to Cuban, we're not in a bubble like the dotcom era—at least not yet—but we are seeing a lot of inflated expectations that could lead to disappointment if AI doesn't deliver on its promises in the near future.

Cuban's perspective is grounded in the belief that AI is part of a long-term technological cycle—a cycle that will take time to mature and fully realize its potential. While the hype and the investments may be premature, he argues that AI's eventual impact on industries and economies will be significant. However, this long-term view doesn't mean we're immune to short-term bubbles. The speculative nature of AI investments, combined with the enormous amounts of money being poured into the sector, creates an environment ripe for a correction.

So, what does the future hold for AI? Will it experience a "bust" like previous tech bubbles? It's difficult to say for certain, but there are clear signs that the AI market is ripe for a reckoning. As we've seen with other technological bubbles, the gap between hype and reality can only be sustained for so long. Eventually, the promises of transformative AI will need to be backed by real-world results, and if they aren't, the industry could experience a sharp downturn.

At the same time, AI has the potential to revolutionize the world in ways we can't yet fully comprehend. It may not happen in the next five years or even ten, but the groundwork is being laid for a future where AI plays a central role in everything from personal assistants to autonomous vehicles to disease diagnosis. The question is whether the current wave of hype will lead to sustainable growth or whether it will burst, leaving investors and companies scrambling to pick up the pieces.

As with any emerging technology, the future of AI is uncertain. What we do know is that the current rush to capitalize on AI's potential—without fully understanding its limitations—could lead to a fallout that mirrors past tech bubbles. Whether we're heading for another dotcom-style crash or whether AI will prove itself as the next great technological revolution, only time will tell. But the stakes are high, and the consequences of overvaluation could be just as painful as those of any previous bubble.

CHAPTER 7

The Real Promise of AI – Can It Live Up to the Hype?

Artificial intelligence is often portrayed as a revolutionary force, capable of transforming entire industries and reshaping the way we live. From self-driving cars to personalized medical treatments, AI promises a future where machines handle tasks once thought to be exclusively human. But while the potential of AI is immense, we must ask: Can AI really live up to the hype? To answer that, we need to take a deeper look at the true potential of AI, its value, and the role it will play in our world.

One of the key areas where AI shows tremendous promise is in cognitive labor—the ability of machines to mimic human decision-making and perform tasks that require intelligence, judgment, and analysis. For years, AI systems have been able to process vast amounts of data far more efficiently than humans ever could. However, what makes AI truly revolutionary is its ability to apply this data to make decisions, offer recommendations, and even predict outcomes.

In industries like finance, AI is already being used to predict stock market trends, optimize trading strategies, and detect fraudulent transactions. In marketing, AI tools analyze customer behavior to predict preferences, segment markets, and tailor advertisements in ways that maximize engagement. In legal work, AI can review documents, search for relevant case law, and even assist in drafting contracts. In each of these examples, AI is not replacing human workers but rather complementing their abilities, performing repetitive tasks with speed and accuracy while leaving the more creative, strategic work to people. This is where AI's value lies—not in replacing human labor but in augmenting it, allowing workers to focus on higher-level tasks that require critical thinking and creativity.

However, the true potential of AI is not limited to just these cognitive tasks. It is poised to play a transformative role in industries like healthcare, education, and entertainment, each of which is in need of innovation and improvement.

In healthcare, AI is already having a significant impact. Machine learning algorithms are being used to analyze medical data and improve diagnostic accuracy, reducing human error and speeding up decision-making. AI-powered systems can scan medical images, identify tumors, and recommend treatments based on vast amounts of data from previous cases. But perhaps one of the most exciting developments is AI's potential to personalize medical treatment. By analyzing genetic data, lifestyle information, and medical history, AI could help doctors create customized treatment plans that are tailored to an individual's unique needs. AI's ability to sift through massive datasets and identify patterns that would be impossible for a human to notice makes it an invaluable tool for doctors and researchers alike. However, it's crucial to understand that AI isn't replacing doctors—it's giving them the ability to make more informed, data-driven decisions that can improve patient outcomes.

In education, AI has the potential to create personalized learning experiences that adapt to each student's needs. Traditional education systems often struggle to meet the individual needs of students, leaving some behind while others coast through without being challenged. AI can bridge this gap by tailoring lessons to the pace and learning style of each student. Imagine a classroom where an AI system tracks a student's progress, identifies areas where they struggle, and adjusts the curriculum to provide targeted support. AI could also help teachers by automating administrative tasks like grading, allowing them to focus more on engaging with students. While AI can certainly enhance educational practices, it's unlikely to replace the role of teachers. Instead, it will serve as an assistant, providing valuable support in ways that help students and educators thrive.

In entertainment, AI is already revolutionizing the way content is created and consumed. Streaming services like Netflix and Spotify use AI algorithms to recommend content based on your viewing or listening history, creating personalized experiences that were once impossible. But AI's role in entertainment goes beyond recommendations. AI is now being used to generate music, write scripts, and even assist in the creation of visual effects. In the future, AI could play a key role in helping creators by suggesting storylines, character arcs, or even dialogue based on patterns in successful content. But like in other industries, the true value of AI in entertainment lies not in replacing human creativity, but in augmenting it—helping artists and creators bring their ideas to life faster and more efficiently.

As we look toward the future, the real promise of AI is in its ability to complement human labor, not replace it. Despite the hype, AI is still far from achieving true general intelligence— machines that can perform any task a human can do. Instead, AI should be viewed as a tool that can enhance human abilities, making our work more efficient, more accurate, and more personalized. In healthcare, AI can help doctors make better decisions. In education, it can help teachers reach every student. In entertainment, it can help creators push the boundaries of what's possible. The key to unlocking AI's true potential lies in how we choose to integrate it into our daily lives and industries.

But the future of AI isn't without its challenges. As AI systems become more integrated into society, questions about ethics, privacy, and the impact on employment will need to be addressed. While AI can automate tasks and make decisions, it still lacks the nuanced understanding and empathy that humans bring to complex situations. The human touch will always be essential in fields like healthcare and education, where personal connection and understanding are key. Additionally, as AI continues to evolve, we must be careful not to overestimate its capabilities or rely too heavily on it in situations where human judgment is irreplaceable.

Looking ahead, the future of AI is one of partnership between humans and machines. The promise of AI is not in replacing us, but in enabling us to do more—whether it's making life-saving medical decisions, creating personalized learning experiences, or enhancing creative expression. The true value of AI lies in its ability to help us unlock our potential, streamline our work, and solve problems that were once beyond our reach.

As AI continues to evolve, we must remain cautious and realistic about its role in society. We must ensure that we use AI responsibly, with a focus on complementing and enhancing human abilities rather than replacing them. The real promise of AI is not in its capacity to think and act like humans, but in its ability to work alongside us, creating a future where technology serves humanity, not the other way around.

CHAPTER 8

AI, Employment, and the Shifting Job Landscape

The rise of artificial intelligence has promised to usher in a new era of progress, where machines handle mundane tasks, enhance efficiency, and open up new frontiers of innovation. But with every technological advancement comes disruption, and AI is no exception. As AI becomes more integrated into various sectors, it is reshaping the world of work in profound ways. While some industries have embraced AI as a tool for progress, others are grappling with the unintended consequences, particularly the displacement of workers and the shifting nature of job roles. The question that arises is whether AI is truly creating a future of abundant opportunities or simply accelerating the displacement of workers across the economy.

Over the past few years, the role of AI in job displacement has become increasingly evident. Tech-related layoffs have dominated headlines from 2022 to 2024, with some of the biggest names in the industry laying off thousands of employees as they embraced AI automation. Companies that once depended on large workforces to manage their operations are now finding that AI can handle many of the tasks that were previously done by humans. For example, AI algorithms are now used to optimize supply chains, analyze financial data, and even create marketing content—all tasks that would have required a team of professionals just a few years ago.

These layoffs are not just limited to the tech industry. AI is having a ripple effect across a wide range of sectors, from finance to manufacturing to retail. As companies adopt AI-driven automation, many workers find themselves out of jobs, unable to compete with machines that can process information faster, more accurately, and without the need for breaks. While the goal of AI is often to improve efficiency and reduce costs, the reality is that for many workers, this has meant a loss of employment opportunities and the need to adapt to an ever-changing job market.

But while AI is undoubtedly causing significant job displacement, it's important to understand the role of AI in job creation as well. Some proponents of AI argue that the technology will not only eliminate jobs but will also create new roles and industries that we can't yet imagine. This vision of a future where AI empowers workers and creates new opportunities is compelling, and indeed, history has shown that technological advancements often lead to the emergence of new industries and job categories.

However, this optimistic view is tempered by the reality that the jobs AI is creating are often highly specialized and require specific skills that many workers do not possess. The shift toward AI-driven automation is leading to an increased demand for AI engineers, data scientists, and other technical roles—positions that require years of training and expertise. While these jobs may provide opportunities for highly skilled workers, they do little to help those who have been displaced by AI and are struggling to find new employment. As a result, the transition to an AI-driven economy may exacerbate income inequality, as the benefits of AI are concentrated in the hands of those who have the skills to thrive in this new landscape.

One of the most controversial impacts of AI is its effect on low-wage workers, particularly in sectors like customer service, office support, and sales. These industries have traditionally relied on large numbers of human workers to handle tasks such as answering customer inquiries, processing transactions, and managing administrative duties. But as AI systems become more sophisticated, these jobs are increasingly being automated. AI-powered chatbots, for example, are replacing customer service representatives, while automated systems are taking over administrative tasks in offices and sales roles in retail.

For low-wage workers, the shift to AI-driven automation is especially concerning. Many of these jobs are vital to the functioning of the economy and provide entry-level opportunities for individuals who lack advanced education or specialized skills. With AI taking over these roles, workers in low-wage industries face an uncertain future, with fewer opportunities for stable, long-term employment. The loss of these jobs has significant social and economic implications, particularly for communities that rely on low-wage work to support their economies.

As AI continues to reshape the job market, companies are reluctant to fully acknowledge the role AI is playing in workforce restructuring. Many companies have been quiet about AI-driven layoffs, preferring to frame them as part of broader cost-cutting measures or efforts to optimize efficiency. For instance, IBM and UPS have both engaged in significant workforce restructuring in recent years, with AI playing a central role in reducing staff. While these companies publicly tout the benefits of AI in improving their operations, they are less willing to acknowledge that the technology has contributed to the layoffs of thousands of workers.

Shopify, another tech giant, has also been accused of using AI in its efforts to reduce its workforce. In 2023, the company quietly laid off a significant number of employees, citing the need to streamline operations and focus on its core business. However, reports suggested that AI systems were playing a significant role in automating tasks that had previously been handled by employees. Shopify's reluctance to openly discuss the impact of AI on its workforce raises questions about the ethical implications of using automation to replace human workers while keeping the public focused on the "positive" aspects of the technology.

The reluctance of companies to openly admit the role of AI in staff reductions highlights a broader issue in the AI discourse. While AI is often framed as a tool that enhances productivity and drives innovation, there is a growing tension between the benefits of automation and its social costs. If companies continue to implement AI-driven layoffs without full transparency, they risk further alienating workers and eroding public trust in both AI and the companies that use it.

As we look ahead, the future of AI and employment is uncertain. The promise of AI as a tool for progress is clear, but so too are the challenges it presents. The key question is how we can ensure that the benefits of AI are shared more equitably, and how we can support workers who are displaced by automation. The rapid pace of AI adoption means that companies, workers, and governments must act quickly to address the potential risks and opportunities of AI. If we don't, we risk creating a world where the benefits of AI are enjoyed by only a few, while the rest of the workforce is left behind.

CHAPTER 9

Preparing for the AI Future – What Consumers and Workers Need to Know

As artificial intelligence continues to permeate every facet of our lives, it's becoming increasingly important for both consumers and workers to approach the rapidly evolving landscape of AI with a **critical mindset**. While AI holds enormous potential to improve our lives, it also comes with its fair share of risks and limitations. Companies, eager to capitalize on the AI boom, often make grandiose claims about their products, promising revolutionary solutions to complex problems. But the reality doesn't always match the hype. As consumers, it's crucial that we learn how to navigate the world of AI, evaluate claims carefully, and understand what we're truly buying into.

How to Critically Assess AI Claims from Companies

The first step in navigating the world of AI hype is to critically assess the claims made by companies. The term "AI" is often thrown around with little explanation of what it actually means or how it works. For many companies, slapping an AI label on a product is a quick and easy way to garner attention, raise stock prices, or appeal to investors. But it's essential to dig deeper and ask the right questions before investing in or purchasing AI-powered products.

Start by asking how the AI actually works. Does the product rely on true machine learning or deep learning algorithms, or is it simply a tool with some basic automation and pattern recognition? Many companies claim their products are AI-driven when, in reality, they are simply using simpler forms of automation that don't involve sophisticated algorithms. Look for specific details about how the AI functions—does it adapt and improve over time, or is it just a static system? Does the company provide transparency about the data that feeds into the system, and how that data is processed and used? If the claims sound too good to be true, they probably are. Don't hesitate to ask for more information and seek out independent reviews and analysis from trusted sources.

Understanding the Limitations and Risks of AI-Powered Products

While AI can certainly be a powerful tool, it's crucial to understand that it has its limitations. AI is not infallible—it can make mistakes, especially when it's confronted with situations that it hasn't been trained to handle. It's also important to note that many AI systems, especially those in their early stages, are still dependent on human oversight and intervention to ensure accuracy.

For instance, in industries like healthcare, AI is being used to assist doctors with diagnostics, but it's not perfect. AI-powered systems can misinterpret medical data, and without a trained medical professional to review the results, errors could occur. AI may be able to process large amounts of data quickly, but it doesn't have the nuanced understanding that human experts bring to complex decisions. The same applies to other fields like finance, legal work, and customer service, where AI can assist with tasks but may struggle with cases that require creative problem-solving or empathy.

Moreover, there are significant risks associated with AI products, particularly in terms of privacy and security. AI systems require vast amounts of data to function effectively, and this data can often include sensitive information. Without proper safeguards in place, this data could be exposed, misused, or exploited. For example, AI-powered recommendation algorithms—used by platforms like social media and e-commerce sites—can lead to echo chambers that reinforce biases and limit exposure to diverse viewpoints. Consumers should be aware of the data privacy policies of companies and how their data will be used, stored, and shared.

What to Watch for in the Fine Print of AI Technology Advertisements

One of the most important things consumers need to pay attention to is the fine print. Just like any other product, AI technology is often accompanied by marketing materials, advertisements, and terms of service agreements that may gloss over important details or bury limitations in small text. Companies are quick to promote the benefits of their AI systems but may downplay the risks or fail to mention the technology's limitations.

Here are some key things to watch for in the fine print:

Data Usage and Privacy: Look for any mention of how your data will be used and whether it will be shared with third parties. Many AI products rely on personal data to function, and it's important to understand who will have access to that information and how it will be protected.

Human Oversight: Companies may claim their AI systems are fully automated, but in reality, human intervention may still be required to ensure accuracy and quality control. If the fine print mentions that the system "requires human oversight," it could be a sign that the product isn't as autonomous as it appears.

Exclusion of Liability: Some companies may include disclaimers in the fine print that limit their liability for errors or failures of their AI systems. For example, if an AI system malfunctions and causes harm or financial loss, the company may claim that they're not responsible. It's essential to understand what protections are in place for consumers in case the AI doesn't perform as expected.

Trial Period and Subscription Costs: Watch for any mention of subscription fees or hidden costs, particularly for AI products that are marketed as "free" or "low-cost." Many AI tools offer a trial period, after which you may be locked into recurring fees that aren't immediately apparent. Always check for any terms regarding ongoing costs or potential future charges.

The Importance of Consumer Awareness and Education

As AI becomes more ubiquitous, it's critical that consumers take an active role in educating themselves about the technology they're using. This means staying informed about the capabilities and limitations of AI systems, reading the fine print, and asking questions when something seems too good to be true. By being discerning and cautious, consumers can better protect themselves from misleading claims and make more informed decisions when interacting with AI-powered products.

In addition to consumers, workers also need to be prepared for the future of AI. It's important for individuals to stay ahead of the curve by learning about the ways AI is changing their industries and acquiring skills that will help them adapt to new technologies. Workers who understand AI's potential—and its limitations—will be better equipped to collaborate with AI systems, rather than be replaced by them.

As AI continues to evolve, the key to navigating this future lies in understanding it—not just as a buzzword, but as a technology that requires careful consideration, transparency, and ethical responsibility. By remaining vigilant, informed, and proactive, we can ensure that AI serves us, rather than the other way around.

Guidance for workers:

As artificial intelligence continues to reshape industries, the job market is undergoing a profound transformation. AI is no longer just a futuristic concept—it's a driving force that is already impacting how work is done, which jobs are in demand, and which roles are at risk of being replaced. For workers, this creates both challenges and opportunities. While some fear that AI will render their skills obsolete, others see it as an opportunity to adapt, grow, and leverage technology to enhance their work. The key to staying relevant in an AI-driven job market lies in understanding how to navigate this shift, reskill, and upskill in ways that complement the growing role of AI.

How to Stay Relevant in an AI-Driven Job Market

Staying relevant in an AI-driven job market requires a mindset shift—one that views AI as a tool that can enhance human work, rather than a force that will replace it entirely.

While AI is certainly capable of performing many tasks traditionally done by humans, it lacks the nuanced understanding, emotional intelligence, and creativity that humans bring to the table. The jobs most at risk of being automated are those that involve repetitive, manual tasks or rely heavily on data processing and basic decision-making.

However, jobs that require problem-solving, critical thinking, and human interaction are less likely to be replaced by AI. For workers, this means focusing on skills that emphasize the uniqueness of human intelligence. Creativity, empathy, leadership, and the ability to collaborate and communicate effectively are all qualities that will remain in high demand, even as AI becomes more advanced.

To stay relevant, workers need to evolve with the times. This means embracing AI as a tool that can help you do your job more effectively, rather than seeing it as a threat. Adaptability is one of the most important skills you can develop. By staying open to new technologies and learning how to work alongside AI, you'll ensure that your career remains relevant, no matter how the landscape changes.

Reskilling and Upskilling in the Age of AI

The rise of AI presents an opportunity for workers to reskill and upskill—in other words, to acquire new skills or deepen existing ones to keep up with the demands of a rapidly changing workforce. In the age of AI, workers can no longer rely solely on their existing skill sets. Instead, they must actively invest in their own learning and development to ensure they remain competitive in a job market that's increasingly driven by automation and advanced technologies.

Reskilling refers to learning new skills that allow you to transition into a different role or industry, especially if your current job is at risk of automation. For example, a customer service representative who is replaced by AI chatbots might consider reskilling to become an AI specialist or a data analyst, learning how to work with AI tools or train AI systems.

Upskilling, on the other hand, involves enhancing your existing skills to make them more relevant in an AI-driven world. For example, if you're a marketing professional, you might consider learning how to use AI-powered analytics tools to better understand customer behavior and improve your campaigns. AI literacy is becoming a crucial skill for nearly every profession, as many industries are incorporating AI into their operations. Upskilling in AI doesn't mean you have to become an AI engineer, but gaining a foundational understanding of how AI works and how it can be applied in your field can help you stay ahead of the curve.

There are a wealth of resources available for workers looking to reskill or upskill. Online platforms like Coursera, edX, and Udacity offer a wide range of courses in areas like AI, machine learning, data analysis, and digital marketing. Many of these courses are designed to be accessible for individuals from all backgrounds, allowing you to build the skills needed to succeed in the AI-driven job market.

It's also important to take advantage of on-the-job training and professional development opportunities offered by employers. Companies that are investing in AI often offer training programs to help their employees learn how to integrate these technologies into their work. This not only benefits the company but also ensures that workers remain engaged, adaptable, and equipped to thrive in a changing environment.

Leveraging AI Tools as a Complement to Human Expertise

One of the most exciting opportunities in the AI-driven job market is the ability for workers to leverage AI tools as a complement to their own expertise. Instead of viewing AI as a competitor, workers can see it as a collaborator—a tool that can help them perform tasks more efficiently and make better decisions.

For example, in healthcare, AI systems can analyze medical data and assist doctors in diagnosing conditions. However, the final decision still rests with the doctor, who uses their expertise, experience, and empathy to guide treatment. Similarly, in education, AI can help personalize learning for students, but it is the teacher who provides the human connection and guidance that is crucial to student success.

Workers in many fields can integrate AI into their daily work to enhance productivity and creativity. A writer might use AI tools to generate ideas or help with research, but it's the writer's unique voice and perspective that makes the content valuable. A graphic designer can use AI to create drafts or automate repetitive design tasks, freeing up more time for creative work. A sales professional can use AI-driven insights to better understand customer preferences and craft more targeted pitches, but their ability to build relationships and close deals remains rooted in human interaction.

The key to leveraging AI is understanding its strengths and limitations and using it as a tool to amplify your own abilities. AI can handle routine, data-driven tasks, but it's the human touch—the creativity, critical thinking, and emotional intelligence—that will always set people apart from machines. By using AI to complement and enhance your expertise, you'll be able to do your job more effectively and focus on the aspects of work that only humans can do.

Preparing for the Future

As AI continues to transform the job market, the most successful workers will be those who embrace change and adapt to new technologies. By reskilling, upskilling, and leveraging AI tools to complement their own expertise, workers can not only survive but thrive in an AI-driven world. The future of work may look different, but it doesn't have to be a dystopian future of mass unemployment. Instead, it can be a future where human creativity and AI innovation work hand-in-hand, creating a more efficient, productive, and fulfilling work environment for all.

The key to navigating the AI future is ongoing learning and adaptability. Those who are willing to evolve with the times and take advantage of the opportunities AI presents will find themselves at the forefront of the next era of work. The future of work may be AI-driven, but it will always be human-centered.

CONCLUSION

The Real AI Revolution – Moving Beyond the Illusion

As we come to the end of this exploration into the world of artificial intelligence, it's clear that AI is not just a passing trend—it's a technology that will shape the future of industries, economies, and societies. But while the promises surrounding AI are undeniably alluring, the reality often falls short of the hype. We've seen how AI has been deceptively marketed, with companies painting a picture of autonomous systems capable of solving every problem, often leaving out the human labor behind the scenes and the limitations of the technology. The hype has created inflated expectations that are simply not yet met by the current state of AI, leading to trust issues and disillusionment as consumers and workers realize that the AI revolution is not as flawless as it's been made out to be.

Throughout this book, we've examined how AI-washing—the practice of exaggerating AI's capabilities to attract investment and attention—has become a pervasive issue. From the Mechanical Turk hoax of the 18th century to Amazon's "Just

Walk Out" system, we've seen how technology can be misrepresented to sell a vision that doesn't align with reality. The consequences of such overhyped promises are serious: they erode trust, mislead consumers, and ultimately, damage the credibility of AI as a whole. As we've discussed, the real-world implications of AI are far more complex than the glossy advertisements suggest, and understanding these complexities is crucial to navigating the AI landscape.

However, despite the risks and disappointments associated with AI, the real promise of AI is still immense. It's important to remember that AI is still in its early stages, and while it may not live up to the fantastical claims of the past, it has the potential to be a transformative force for good. AI can enhance human labor, empower workers, and solve problems that were once considered intractable. From healthcare to education to entertainment, AI has already begun to make meaningful contributions, helping to personalize experiences, optimize processes, and improve outcomes. But for AI to truly reach its potential, we must approach it with a realistic understanding of what it can and cannot do.

Looking to the future, AI should be viewed as a tool, not a replacement for human ingenuity. It should complement our abilities, helping us make better decisions, freeing us from mundane tasks, and empowering us to be more creative and productive. AI has the potential to improve our lives, but it needs to be properly understood and applied. The key is not in pushing AI as a catch-all solution, but in using it where it makes sense, while recognizing that human expertise, empathy, and creativity remain irreplaceable.

Now, more than ever, it's critical for consumers, workers, and societies to question the hype. We must demand transparency from the companies that create AI products, understanding how the technology works, who is behind it, and what the limitations are. We must move beyond the marketing and recognize AI for what it truly is: a tool with immense potential, but one that is still evolving. By understanding AI's capabilities—and its limitations—we can harness it for the benefit of society, ensuring that its development is ethical, transparent, and equitable.

As we stand on the cusp of this new technological era, we have a choice: to be swept up in the wave of AI hype and overpromise, or to move forward with a clear-eyed, thoughtful approach that considers the implications of this technology for all of us. The AI revolution, if managed responsibly, can be a force for progress. But it requires that we approach it with caution, responsibility, and a commitment to understanding its true potential.

The future of AI is in our hands. It's up to us to question the narrative, demand honesty, and make sure that AI serves humanity—not the other way around.